Bob Chilcott
Carols 1

9 carols for mixed voices

MUSIC DEPARTMENT

OXFORD
UNIVERSITY PRESS

OXFORD
UNIVERSITY PRESS

Great Clarendon Street, Oxford OX2 6DP, England
198 Madison Avenue, New York, NY10016, USA

Oxford University Press is a department of the University of Oxford.
It furthers the University's aim of excellence in research, scholarship,
and education by publishing worldwide

13

ISBN 0-19-353233-6   978-0-19-353233-5

Music and text origination by Barnes Music Engraving Ltd., East Sussex
Printed in the United Kingdom on acid-free paper by
Halstan Printing Group, Amersham.

Contents

Preface

These nine pieces represent almost all of the mixed-voice carols I have written over the last ten years. The first to appear, *Mid-winter*, was originally written in 1994 as an upper-voice carol for the Toronto Children's Chorus, but is included here in a version for mixed voices. Most of the texts for these pieces will be well known and loved by choir singers, but I hope that one or two will be new, among them the folk-like text of *The Shepherd's Carol* which was suggested by the Dean of King's College, Cambridge. It was at the service where this was first sung that I heard a reading of the beautiful Elizabeth Jennings poem used here in *For Him all Stars have Shone*. Another woman poet, the American Janet Lewis, is represented in the gentle and human poem *Christmas-tide*, and the text of *The Time of Snow* is mine.

I would like to thank Robin Barry, who has encouraged so much of the work in this book.

Bob Chilcott
May 2004

for Joanne Hart

Christmas-tide

Janet Lewis (1899–1998)

BOB CHILCOTT (b. 1955)

Also available separately: BC15; ISBN 978-0-19-343218-5

Text reproduced by permission of Ohio University Press
This piece © Oxford University Press 1997 and 2004
This collection © Oxford University Press 2004

Printed in Great Britain

OXFORD UNIVERSITY PRESS MUSIC DEPARTMENT, GREAT CLARENDON STREET, OXFORD OX2 6DP

an-gel came   to   pro-phe-sy His name?   Ah   no,   not so,   she

could   not love Him more,   but   loved Him just the same.____

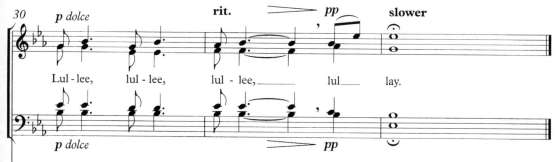

Lul - lee,   lul - lee,   lul - lee,____   lul____   lay.

*Commissioned by the Cheyenne Chamber Singers for the Cheyenne Chamber Singers
and the All-City Children's Chorus, conductor Jane Iverson*

For Him all Stars have Shone

Elizabeth Jennings (1926–2001)

BOB CHILCOTT (b. 1955)

Also available separately: BC57; ISBN 978-0-19-343301-4. The upper-voice part to this arrangement is available as a separate leaflet: ISBN 978-0-19-343335-9. A version for 4-part upper voices and piano appears in *For Him all Stars: 15 carols for upper voices*: ISBN 978-0-19-335569-9

Text by Elizabeth Jennings; by permission of David Higham Associates.

And care-ful shep - herds   look u - pon   the   one   un-sul - lied

TUTTI

mp espress.   *div.*

birth.   They   kneel   and_   stare___   while time   seems gone___   and

mp espress.

rit.   **a tempo**

unis.

good-ness rules   the earth.

mp più espress.

for Michael Kibblewhite and Cantate Youth Choir

Lully, lulla, thou little tiny child

15th century

BOB CHILCOTT (b. 1955)

Mid-winter

Christina Rossetti (1830–94)

BOB CHILCOTT (b. 1955)

Also available separately: BC3; ISBN 978-0-19-343194-2 and in a version for upper voices and piano: BC1; ISBN 978-0-19-341523-2
2 different orchestral accompaniments are available for rental. Brass: 2tpt, hn, tbn, tba, hp, pno Orchestra: 2fl, 2ob, 2cl. 2bsn, 2hn, hp, str

God, heav'n can - not hold him nor_ earth sus - tain:

Heav'n and earth shall flee a-way when he comes to reign:

In the bleak mid - win - ter a sta - ble - place, a place_ suf - ficed_

place_ suf - ficed_____ The_

air; But on-ly his mo - ther in her mai - - den bliss Wor-shipped the be -lo - ved with a kiss.

SOPRANO & ALTO *unis.* **p** *dolce*

What_ can I give_ him,

poor_ as I am? If I were a

shep - herd I would bring a lamb;

for David Hill and The Bach Choir
in celebration of the 80th Birthday of Sir David Willcocks

Nova! nova!

15th century (slightly modernized)

BOB CHILCOTT (b. 1955)

[1] *Nova! nova! 'Ave' fit ex 'Eva'. = News! news! 'Ave' ('hail') is made from 'Eva' ('Eve').*

First appeared in *Advent for Choirs* edited by Malcolm Archer and Stephen Cleobury (ISBN 978-0-19-353025-6). Also available separately: BC46; ISBN 978-0-19-343300-7

² I-wys = indeed ³ wened = thought

for Gillian Dibden and the Berkshire Youth Choir

Remember, O thou man

Thomas Ravenscroft? (*c*.1582–1635)

BOB CHILCOTT (b. 1955)

Also available separately BC89; ISBN 978-0-19-335635-1.
First appeared in *Christmas Spirituals for Choirs* compiled by Bob Chilcott and Ken Burton (ISBN 978-0-19-343541-4)

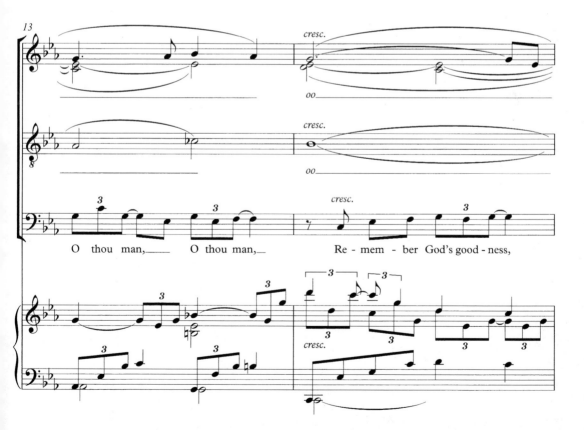

On heav'ns high hill!_____ The an - gels all did sing_____

prai - ses._____ to our heav'n - ly King,

and peace to man li - ving___ with a good will.___

To Beth - lem did they go,___

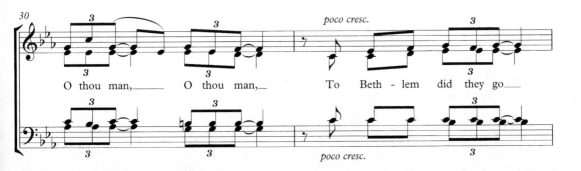

O thou man,___ O thou man,___ To Beth - lem did they go___

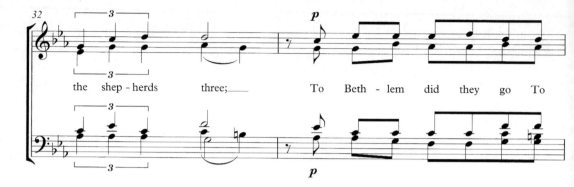

the shep - herds three;___ To Beth - lem did they go To

see whe - ther it were so,___ whe - ther Christ was born or no___ to set man

free,___ to set man free.___

for Stephen Cleobury and the Choir of King's College, Cambridge

The Shepherd's Carol

Clive Sansom (1910-81)

BOB CHILCOTT (b. 1955)

Also available separately: BC44; ISBN 978-0-19-343296-3

13

Si-lence more love - ly than   mu - sic____

calm,_____   Si-lence more love - ly than   mu - sic____

Si - lence,   si - -   lence,_____

calm,_____   Si - lence,_

pp

still,_____   Si-lence more love - ly than   mu - sic____

pp

Si - -   lence,_____

pp

Si - -   lence,_____   si - -

pp

23
cresc. *mf* *f*
Larg-er than Ve-nus it was and bright, so bright. Oh, a
cresc. *mf* *f*
Lar-ger than Ve-nus it was and bright, so bright. Oh, a
cresc. *mf* *f*
Lar-ger than Ve-nus it was and bright, so bright. Oh, a
cresc. *mf* *f*
and bright, so bright. Oh, a

cresc. *mf* *f*

26
ff appass.
voice from the sky, La-dy, It seemed to us then
ff appass.
voice from the sky, La-dy, It seemed to us then
ff appass.
voice from the sky, La-dy, It seemed to us then
ff appass.
voice from the sky, La-dy, It seemed to us then

ff appass.

so we have come, La - dy, Our day's work done, Our

Our

love,__ our hopes, our - selves__ we give to your son.__

Love,__ our - selves__ La - dy,

love,__ our hopes, our - selves__ La - dy,

Love,__ our - selves__ La - dy,

Love,__ our - selves__ La - dy, La -

The Time of Snow

BOB CHILCOTT (b. 1955)

They jour-ney on-ward to find___ their rest,

Also available separately: BC56; ISBN 978-0-19-343312-0, and in a version for upper voices and piano; BC21; ISBN 978-0-19-342632-0
An orchestral accompaniment is available for rental. Hp, 2perc [susp cymb / glock, and triangle], str

Ma-ry and Jo - seph, for e - ver blessed.

TENOR They

S. They tra-vel wea - ri - ly___ as they go, the time___ of win - ter, the

A. They tra - vel wea-ry as they go,___ the time,

T. tra - vel wea - ri - ly___ as they go, the time,___ the

B. They tra - vel as they go,

time___ of win - ter, the   time___   of   snow.

the time,   the time   of   snow.

the   time,___ the   time   of   snow.

the time   of   snow.

p

mp cresc.

It may not   have been win-ter then,

mp cresc.

mp sonore

that cer-tain night in Beth-le - hem,___ but with the beau-ty of this birth came

the re - new - al of the earth, of the earth,

as a flower that grows____

through the melt - ing

snows.

There in the si - lence lies Ma - ry's

son,

a source of won - der for

S. ev - ery - one.   With-in a sta - ble so

A. ev - ery - one.   A sta - ble so

T. ev - ery - one.   With - in a sta - ble

B. ev - ery - one.   A sta - ble so

poco cresc.

for Michael Kibblewhite and Cantate Youth Choir

Where Riches is Everlastingly

16th century (adapted B.C.)

BOB CHILCOTT (b. 1955)

The percussion parts are available to purchase separately from the publisher; ISBN 978-0-19-355845-8

pray you be mer - ry   and   sing   with_ me   In   wor-ship of Christ's na - ti -

pray you be mer - ry   and   sing   with me   In   wor-ship of Christ's na - ti -

na - ti -

- vi - ty.

- vi-ty.   *Lall   lall lall_ lall   lall___ lall   lall lall   lall   Lall   lall lall_ lall   lall*

- vi - ty.

57 Lall lall lall lall lall lall lall lall lall Lall lall lall lall lall lall lall la I
poor clothes was wrapped the Lord Al-migh - ty. I
Lall lall lall lall lall lall lall lall lall Lall lall lall lall lall lall lall la I
poor clothes was wrapped the Lord Al-migh - ty.

61 pray you be mer - ry and sing with me In wor-ship of Christ's na - ti - vi - ty. I
pray you be mer - ry and sing with me In wor-ship of Christ's na - ti - vi - ty. I
I

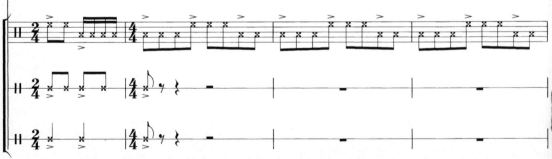

wor-ship of Christ's na - ti - vi - ty. I pray you be mer-ry and sing with me In

wor-ship of Christ's na - ti - vi - ty. I pray you be mer-ry and sing with me In

wor-ship of Christ's na - ti - vi - ty.

wor-ship of Christ's na - ti - vi - ty.